D0365040

To Our Parents

Unless otherwise indicated, Scripture is from the Holy Bible: New International Version, copyright 1973, 1978, 1984 by the International Bible Society. Used by permission of Zondervan Bible Publishers.

Scripture references marked TLB are from The Living Bible, copyright 1971 by Tyndale House Publishers, Wheaton, Ill. Used by permission.

Published by Multnomah Press
Portland, Oregon 97266

Printed in Hong Kong

Library of Congress Cataloging-in-Publication Data

Sattgast, L. J., 1953-
Teach me about the Bible / by L.J. Sattgast and Jan Elkins ; illustrated by Russ Flint.
p. cm.
Summary: Identifies the Bible as God's word and discusses some of the stories that can be found in it.
ISBN 0-88070-385-7
1. Bible—Juvenile literature. [1. Bible] I. Elkins, Jan. II. Flint, Russ, ill. III. Bible. English. Selections. 1990. IV. Title
BS539.S25 1990
220—dc20

90-33886
CIP
AC

91 92 93 94 95 96 97 98 99 - 9 8 7 6 5 4 3 2

By L.J. Sattgast & Jan Elkins

Illustrations by Russ Flint

MULTNOMAH

Portland, Oregon 97266

Books! Books!

Look at all my books!

Can you guess which one

is my favorite book?

Here it is!

The Bible is my favorite book.

The Bible is God's Word,

and every word in the Bible

is true. I listen to a story from

the Bible every day.

All Scripture is God-breathed and is useful for teaching, rebuking, correcting and training in righteousness. . . (2 Timothy 3:16).

BIBLE

The Bible tells me about God. God made the world and everything in it. He takes care of me day and night.

My help comes from the L*ORD, the Maker of heaven and earth (Psalm 121:2).*

The Bible tells me about Jesus.

Jesus is God's Son.

He came to tell people about God.

Now this is eternal life: that they may know you, the only true God, and Jesus Christ, whom you have sent (John 17:3).

The Bible tells me about the Holy Spirit. God sent the Holy Spirit to live with us.

I can't see the Holy Spirit, but he helps me to be kind and good.

The Holy Spirit ... will teach you all things and will remind you of everything I have said to you (John 14:26).

I learn about God's promises in the Bible. When I see a rainbow, I remember that God kept his promise to Noah, and he will keep his promises to me.

For I will see the rainbow in the cloud and remember my eternal promise to every living being on the earth (Genesis 9:16, TLB).

I like to hear Bible stories about
people who loved God.
I want to love and obey God like
King David and Queen Esther.

The Bible tells me that Jesus obeyed his mother and father. I want to obey my parents too.

Then he went down to Nazareth with [Joseph and Mary] and was obedient to them (Luke 2:51).

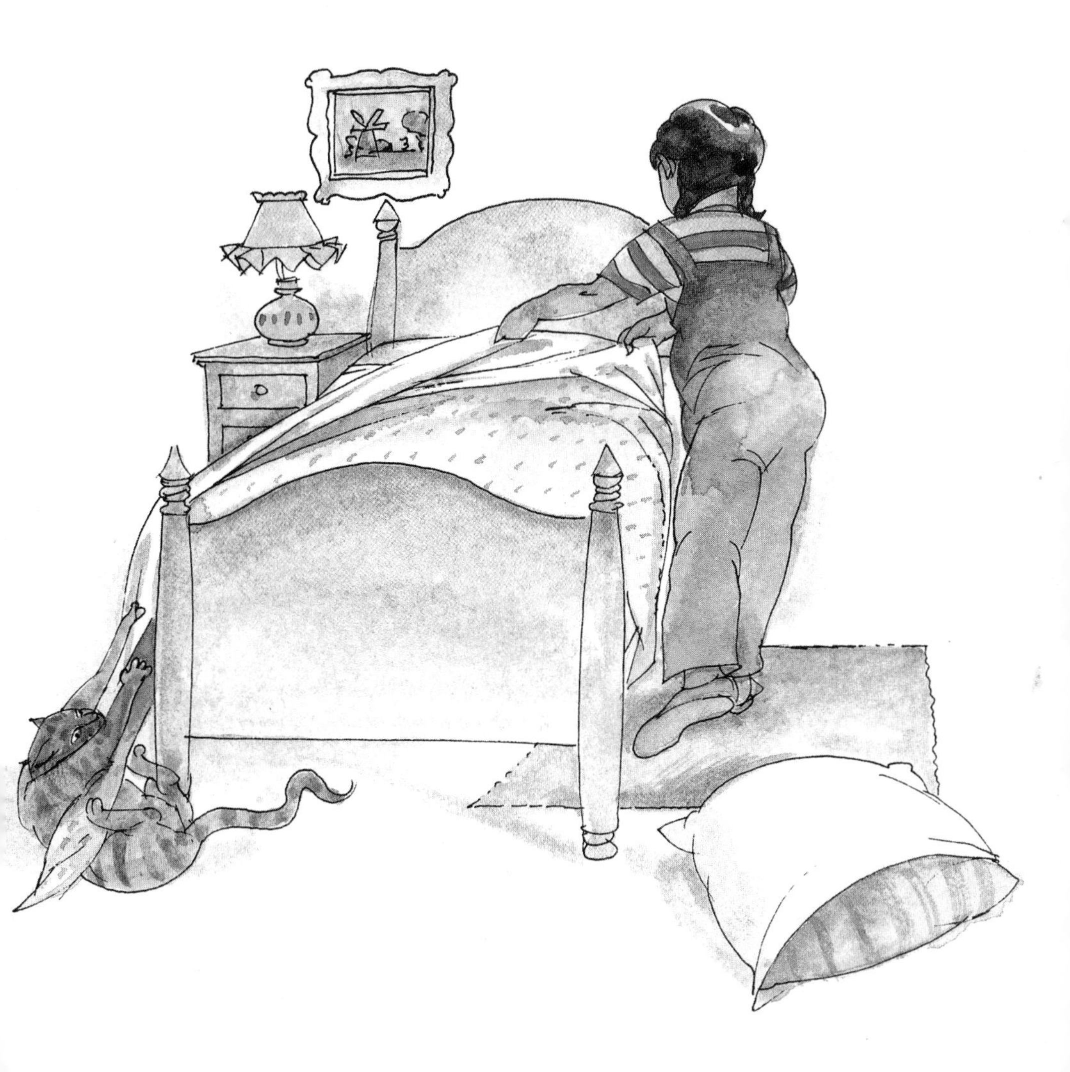

The Bible says to take care
of your animals.
I take good care of my kitty.

A righteous man cares for the needs of his animal . . .
(Proverbs 12:10).

The Bible shows me what I should do. It is like a light that shines on my path.

Your word is a lamp to my feet and a light for my path (Psalm 119:105).

Things around us don't last.

But God's Word will last forever!

Your word, O LORD, is eternal; it stands firm in the heavens (Psalm 119:89).

Helpful hints for parents about the

BIBLE

IMPORTANCE OF THE BIBLE

Your child needs to know that:

- The Bible is the Word of God. To love and obey God, your child must know what God says in his Word.
- He needs to "plant the Word of God in his heart." As he grows, he will realize more and more that God's Word is a necessity, like air and food.
- She needs to apply biblical principles to her thoughts, words, and actions.

YOUR ATTITUDE TOWARD THE BIBLE

- Read the Word of God daily and ask God to make it precious to you.
- Your child will learn that the Bible is special by how often you read it, talk about it, and relate it to your life.
- Ask the Lord for specific wisdom on how to begin training your child.

CHOOSING A BIBLE

There are many children's Bibles available. Look for one that has:

- Fairly simple words and sentences (compare with other books your child enjoys reading).
- Lots of bright, colorful, lively pictures.
- A storybook style—short block of text with each picture.

PROCEDURE

- Set aside a special time for Bible reading with your child—a close, intimate, undisturbed time.
- Make it fun and keep it short, rather than a time to be endured.
- Help your child apply Bible truths at his level.
- Be consistent. Have a "Bible Time" with your child on a daily basis. You will be teaching her to have devotions on her own when she is older.

FOLLOW-UP

- Have your child tell you something he has learned. See what is sinking into his understanding and what is not.
- If your plan isn't working, don't be afraid to start over and try something new.

- Encourage your child. She will not be able to grasp truths except through repetition, time, and experience.

SCRIPTURE MEMORIZATION

Helping your child memorize Scripture is a great privilege. You will be storing up treasures of truth, hope, and life in your child's heart!

- Use simple, easy-to-understand verses to memorize.
- Keep track of the verses on Sunday school papers and repeat them throughout the week.
- Say verses out loud during routine activities such as bath time, play time, or riding in the car.
- Say a verse at the dinner table before praying, or review a verse before your child goes to bed.
- Write a verse on a piece of paper and have your child draw a picture of what it means to him. Display the art.
- Make up a song to help your child remember a verse, or purchase books and tapes that set Scripture to music.

ADDITIONAL SUGGESTIONS

- Read Bible stories with expression—a smile, a frown, snoring, etc.
- Have a question-and-answer time to help your child remember the story.
- Act out Bible stories and parables.
- Use ordinary objects around the house or outside to teach Bible truths, e.g., when you see birds, talk about how God takes care of them and how he takes care of us too (Matthew 10).
- Buy or make a puppet. Use it to tell stories that illustrate Bible truths.
- Purchase flannelgraph stories or make your own figures from Sunday school papers. (Cut out and glue a strip of flannel on the back.) Let your child help you move the figures around on the board. As she gets older, she will be able to tell the stories herself.